BRITAIN IN OLD PHOTOGRAPHS

WESTMINSTER

JILL BARBER

CITY OF WESTMINSTER

SUTTON PUBLISHING LIMITED

Sutton Publishing Limited
Phoenix Mill · Thrupp · Stroud
Gloucestershire · GL5 2BU

British Library Cataloguing in Publication Data
A catalogue record for this book is available from the
British Library.

First published 1998

ISBN 0-7509-1721-0

Copyright © Jill Barber and City of
Westminster Archives Centre, 1998

Title page: Victoria Street, 1892. *See* p. 9.

Typeset in 10/12 Perpetua.
Typesetting and origination by
Sutton Publishing Limited.
Printed in Great Britain by
Ebenezer Baylis, Worcester.

WESTMINSTER CITY ARCHIVES

The purpose-built City of Westminster Archives Centre opened in 1995, bringing together a vast collection of printed and documentary material relating to the history of Westminster, Marylebone and Paddington. This collection includes a copy of every important book on London, and some 50,000 photographs, prints, watercolours and drawings — a uniquely valuable record of the buildings and people of Westminster from 1650 to the present day. The earliest original document dates from 1256, and there is a particularly fine collection of maps and plans. A special theatre collection covers all West End theatres from the eighteenth century onwards. The Centre is keen to promote access to this treasure store through work with schools, adult education classes and publications. For further information please contact Westminster City Archives, 10 St Ann's Street, London SW1P 2XR (Tel: 0171 641 5180).

ACKNOWLEDGEMENTS

All of the photographs in this book have come from the collection held at the City of Westminster Archive Centre where they may be seen without appointment during opening hours. Many of the photographs have been given or loaned to the collection by private individuals, schools and businesses. I would like to thank the following for permission to reproduce images used in this book: Associated Press, Burdett-Coutts Primary School, The Grey Coat Hospital, Bishop's Move, A. Elliott, John Lobb Ltd, Liberty Plc, London Transport Museum, Sport and General Press Agency, Mr and Mrs P.J. Underwood, F.J. Watson.

I would also like to thank all my colleagues at the City of Westminster Archives Centre, whose expertise has helped me to solve the many puzzles which arose over the identification of buildings that have disappeared and photographs which were not what they seemed!

CONTENTS

INTRODUCTION

Westminster has always been an historic city. Of national, not just local importance, it has long held the law courts and royal palaces within its boundaries, and remains today the seat of government. The Abbey, from which it takes its name, is over 900 years old, and continues to play a dominant part in the life of the nation.

Originally, Westminster was the name given to the marshy area around Thorney Island, nicknamed 'the Devil's Acre' by Dickens in 1859 because of the notorious slums which sprang up in the shadows of the Abbey. As the area west of the City of London began to expand in the seventeenth century, the name began to be applied to a wider area, culminating in 1900 in the creation of the borough of Westminster. This area, from Knightsbridge in the west to the Strand in the east, encompassing Pimlico, Victoria, Mayfair, Soho, Covent Garden, St Clement Danes and Piccadilly, is the Westminster of this book. In 1965 Westminster expanded again, the present City of Westminster including St Marylebone and Paddington, but these areas have not been included here. As it is, the wealth of photographic evidence for this historic area is such that far more has had to be excluded than could possibly be included.

The earliest photographic studios in England were situated in Regent Street and there are some surprisingly early views of Westminster in the 1860s and '70s before the great changes of the late Victorian and Edwardian periods. In many cases whole streets have disappeared, not just the buildings within them, so these images give a unique opportunity to see an earlier pattern. Westminster has always been a centre for tourists and within its boundaries may be found a wealth of buildings and monuments of architectural, historical and social interest, which have changed little, although their surroundings may now be very different.

Theatres remain a characteristic feature of the West End. Many of the small nineteenth-century theatres and music-halls have disappeared, but included here are some of the forgotten names who thrilled audiences of their day. Shopping also has strong associations with Westminster from Nash's Regent Street which created the most fashionable shops in London, to the largest fruit, flower and vegetable market at Covent Garden. Developments in transport, which transformed Westminster both physically and socially during the nineteenth century, can be seen in images which include a failed tram experiment in 1861. More recent has been the impact of the Second World War on Westminster. Some of the devastation caused by intensive bombing can be seen, together with the disruption to people's everyday lives and an insight into some of the emotions running high at the time.

The population of Westminster has always been very mixed, the housing developments of the nineteenth century including both artisans' dwellings and mansion flats. In this selection, however, an inevitable bias to the rich may be detected, as it was frequently the grandest buildings and the most opulent interiors that caught the photographer's eye.

CHAPTER ONE

PLACES OF INTEREST

The Eleanor cross, seen here about 1870 in the forecourt of Charing Cross station, is a replica of the original which marked the resting place of Edward I's Queen before her burial in Westminster Abbey. Charing Cross station opened in 1864 on the site of the old Hungerford Market. Designed by A.S. Barry and based on drawings of the original, the cross cost the railway company £1,800. The first Eleanor Cross (from which Charing Cross takes its name) was erected in 1290 where the statue of Charles I stands today in Trafalgar Square. It was pulled down in 1647 on the orders of Parliament but was already in a ruinous state.

Dating from the 1860s, these two views provide the earliest photographic record of one of London's most visited areas, the southern end of Trafalgar Square. The statue of Charles I on horseback, facing towards the place of his execution in Whitehall, was erected in 1660 on the site where the original Charing Cross stood until 1647. The statue, completed by Le Suear in 1632, was miraculously hidden during the Civil War in the crypt of St Paul's Covent Garden and presented to Charles II on his restoration.

The lion on the arch over the main gateway of Northumberland House, seen here, was erected in 1749. Built about 1610 for the Earl of Northumberland, by the middle of the nineteenth century this was the sole survivor of the mansions which once lay between the Strand and the Thames. Demolished in 1874, despite much protest, to make way for Northumberland Avenue, the Percy lion was removed to Syon House.

Each of the palaces along the Strand had its own gateway to the river where its owners could board their private barges. Photographed in 1886, this is all that remains of York House, now separated from the Thames by the Embankment, built between 1864 and 1870. York House, built before 1237, was demolished in the 1670s. This water-gate was added in 1626 by George Villiers, Duke of Buckingham, during his residence here. The Villiers coat of arms can be seen, and the lions holding shields with anchors symbolize Buckingham's service as Lord High Admiral.

Cleopatra's Needle stands nearly 60 ft high and weighs about 186 tons. Made of granite, the obelisk was transported down the Nile to Heliopolis in about 1475 BC and later moved to Alexandria. Originally dedicated to Tethmosis III, the name Cleopatra was a later addition. Presented to the British in 1819, it was impossible to move it to England until 1878 when a cylindrical iron pontoon was designed to tow it by sea. It was originally intended to be erected in front of the Houses of Parliament but stands today on the Embankment, where it can be seen here in 1920.

St Stephen's Tower, seen here about 1922, is better known as 'Big Ben'. The name was originally given to the great bell erected in 1858 and commemorates local hero Benjamin Caunt, prizefighter and landlord of the Coach and Horses in St Martin's Lane who fought an epic 60 rounds in September 1857. The clock tower was part of the rebuilding of the Houses of Parliament after the disastrous fire of 1834.

The north door of Westminster Abbey, 1870. It remains little changed, apart from the traffic which now thunders past. Nothing remains of Edward I's eleventh-century church, which was rebuilt by Henry III, between 1245 and 1272. His mason was a Frenchman, whose influence can be seen in the rose windows and flying buttresses.

The Clock Tower, Victoria Station, S. W. London.

'Little Ben', a cast iron replica of St Stephen's Tower, c. 1900. It was donated to Westminster City Council by S. Smith and Sons of Clerkenwell and erected at the approach to Victoria Station in 1892. Removed for road widening in 1964, it was replaced in 1981 to commemorate the Royal Wedding.

The vision for a Roman Catholic Cathedral in Westminster became a reality when Cardinal Manning bought the land, just south of Victoria Street, in 1884. Originally marshland, the site had been occupied since 1826 by the Bridewell, a women's prison. The original design for a Gothic cathedral by Henry Clutton was abandoned due to lack of funds, and replaced with a Byzantine design by J.F. Bentley, appointed in 1892 by Archbishop Henry Vaughan. The building was completed in 1903, about the time this picture was taken, revealing 'building plots' still for sale in the foreground

This site in the Strand – then an insalubrious slum – was bought in 1865 for £1,453,000, to bring together all the superior courts concerned with civil, rather than criminal, cases. G.E. Street was appointed architect but a combination of labour troubles, bad weather and financial difficulties meant that although the building was begun in 1871, it was not completed until 1882. The stress of the project contributed to Street's death in 1881 and his statue is in the main hall. The building, seen here about 1890, contained nineteen courts but was extended in 1911 to provide four more and again in 1968.

York House, one of the great Pall Mall mansions, was built in the early 1760s by Matthew Brettingham for the Duke of York, the brother of George III. Renamed Cumberland House, it was refurbished by Robert Adam in the 1780s when it passed to the Duke's brother. In 1807 it became the home of the War Office, which remained there until it moved to its new building in Whitehall in 1906. Sadly, the house was demolished in 1908.

Named in honour of the famous battle of 1815, Waterloo Place was begun the following year to provide a view of Carlton House (the Prince Regent's residence) in Pall Mall from Nash's Regent Street. The Crimea Memorial is today dwarfed by the rebuilding of the northern end which dates from the period 1902 to 1925, but here in about 1880 it still holds its own.

The Strand in 1911 with the north side, where Bush House now stands, in process of being demolished. The elegant church of St Mary-le-Strand was rebuilt by James Gibbs between 1714 and 1717, an earlier medieval church having been demolished in 1549. The architect had recently returned from Rome, and the influence of sixteenth-century Italian architecture can be seen here. The Gaiety theatre is on the left.

St George Hanover Square has been the scene of fashionable weddings since its completion in 1724; Theodore Roosevelt was one of the many famous people to marry there. Designed by John James, it boasts the earliest full-scale Corinthian portico in London. Originally in the parish of St Martin in the Fields, the new church was needed to cope with the rapidly growing population west of the City. It is seen here about 1915.

St John's Smith Square, looking from Millbank down Dean Stanley Street, which was called Church Street at the time this photograph was taken in 1892. Designed by Thomas Archer in the baroque style, it was completed in 1728 after starting to sink into the marshy ground beneath. It was never popular, described by Charles Dickens as 'some petrified monster, frightful and gigantic, on its back with its legs in the air'. It was bombed in 1941 but was painstakingly restored in the 1960s as a concert hall.

'The handsomest barn in England', is how Inigo Jones described St Paul's Covent Garden, which he built in 1631 for the Earl of Bedford, who did not want to be put to great expense on a church to go with his new development. Seen here about 1935, today it is known as the 'Actors Church', not only because of the number of famous actors who have been buried here but also because it is adjacent to Drury Lane, which used to be the centre of theatreland. It remains the earliest classical parish church in England.

The entrance gate of Millbank Prison, Grosvenor Road, is seen here in 1892 shortly before its demolition. The penitentiary was vast and intimidating, and the site was chosen partly for its isolation. Jeremy Bentham's experimental scheme, aimed at reform, ran into trouble from the outset: the first prisoners arrived in 1816 but in 1823 the prison had to be evacuated because of the outbreak of disease. By 1843 it was clear that the reformatory experiment had failed, and Millbank became a centre for those awaiting transportation. It ended its days as a women's prison, closing in 1890. Part of this site is now occupied by the Tate Gallery.

Caxton Hall, seen here in 1924, was designed by Lee and Smith and opened as Westminster's City Hall in 1883. It was used by the suffragettes at the beginning of the century and Sir Winston Churchill spoke here during the Second World War. It became a register office in 1933 and has hosted marriages of the rich and famous including Elizabeth Taylor, Ingrid Bergman, Ringo Starr, Diana Dors (twice) and Peter Sellars. Having had a glorious past, its future remains uncertain.

CHAPTER TWO

STREET SCENES

It is hard to believe that the Strand can be glimpsed in the distance of this peaceful scene, taken on 1 July 1898 before the car took over the streets. On the right, a milk delivery is taking place in Craven Street, where several eighteenth-century terraced houses remain. Northumberland Avenue, to the left, was built in 1876, and contained several smart hotels, now taken over as offices.

The east side of Parliament Street, about 1876. There was a bank at no. 55, next door to John Rorke's gallery. At no. 53, where Isambard Kingdom Brunel had his office in the 1830s, there was Thomas Whitmore's fruit shop and Charles Baker's restaurant. This was rebuilt in 1896. A penny farthing is leaning against the shop at the right of the picture.

Bridge Street in 1870, with Cannon Row on the right, a narrow alley described by Dickens in *Nicholas Nickleby* as a 'street of gloomy lodging houses . . . a sanctuary of Smaller Members of Parliament. . . . There are legislators in the parlours, in the first floor, in the second, in the third, in the garrets; the small apartments reek with the breath of deputations and delegates.'

Princes Street from Broad Sanctuary, *c.* 1870. The railings to the left are those of the monument to the old boys of Westminster School who fell in the Crimea and the Indian Mutiny which stands at the archway entrance to Dean's Yard. The Royal Aquarium was built on this site in 1875 and replaced by Westminster Methodist Central Hall in 1903.

Whitehall, 1884. Much of this area was rebuilt as government offices around 1910.

Millbank Street, looking north, *c.* 1863, before the houses on the right were demolished to make way for Victoria Tower Gardens.

Thames Parade, Grosvenor Road, *c.* 1870. Built by John Johnson in the early 1820s, this pleasant row of stucco houses is all that survives of the earliest phase of building on Millbank. On the right is the iron church of All Saint's. Built in 1860 as a temporary structure, it was rebuilt in 1871 and finally demolished in 1974.

Millbank in 1870, looking north from the Speaker's stables. On the left can be seen the grim entrance to Millbank prison, guarded by a lone policeman. It closed in 1890, and was demolished in 1903. Millbank, described by Dickens as 'a melancholy waste', takes its name from the fourteenth-century mill built by the Abbots of Westminster, which survived until the early eighteenth century.

Grosvenor Crescent, *c.* 1900. The name of this beautiful Georgian street is a reminder that for over 300 years the Grosvenor family have owned some of the most valuable land in Westminster. Mayfair was the first to be developed (1720–70), followed by Belgravia in the 1820s and finally Pimlico.

Regent Street, 1916. Once the fashionable shopping street of the aristocracy, by this time it was attracting the middle classes from all over London. It was redeveloped in the 1920s.

Oxford Street, 1895. Built as a residential area in the eighteenth century, in the late nineteenth century it began to develop into the shopping street it is today. It is seen here at a crucial point of change, just before the Act of 1896 which brought the motor car on to the streets. Notice the wide variety of public, private and commercial transport.

Traffic at the junction of the Aldwych and the Strand, May 1910. Horses and motors ran side by side and crossing the road seems to have been a dangerous activity. The Aldwych was officially opened in 1905, the name 'Aldwic' being the old Saxon name for this area – still in use in 1398 – and the original name of Drury Lane.

Pall Mall from the corner of St James's Street, *c.* 1890. An architect's nightmare – notice the lack of windows in the building on the right – because it overlooked the private grounds of Marlborough House, the home of the Prince of Wales from 1863. The gates can be seen here before they were moved back to their present position in 1928. Designed by Thomas Dudley in 1875 for the Junior Naval and Military Club, a succession of clubs followed before it was demolished in 1930. The building on the left was designed by Norman Shaw in 1882.

The Strand, looking east from the corner of Savoy Street, 1885. Advertisements can be seen for *Arrah-Na-Pogue*, which opened at the Adelphi Theatre on 25 July 1885, and *It's Never too Late to Mend*, which played at Drury Lane in July 1885. Shops on the south side include at no. 126 Richard Starkie, chemist and druggist, and Charles Boswell, gunmaker, with Gilbert Stanton, surgeon dentist, at no. 128.

Leicester Square, *c.* 1900. The car outside the Hotel Cavour, on the left, is attracting obvious interest. Next door, at no. 22, is George Withers and Sons, musical instrument makers, while beyond lies the impressive frontage of the Alhambra music-hall. Opened in 1858, replacing the short-lived Royal Panoptican, the Alhambra was rebuilt in 1883 after being destroyed by fire. It was demolished in 1936 and this is now the site of the Odeon Cinema.

Piccadilly, *c.* 1898. Green Park, on the right, is said to have been the burial ground of the lepers from the hospital of St James, which is supposedly why there are no flowers here. It was enclosed by Henry VIII and made into a royal park by Charles II. In the eighteenth century it was a favourite place for duels.

Piccadilly, showing Prince's restaurant on the right, *c.* 1902. Building began here in the early seventeenth century when a tailor, who had made a fortune out of 'picadils', a type of stiff collar then fashionable at court, bought some land and built himself a country house which was promptly nicknamed 'Piccadilly Hall'.

Clarges Street, Piccadilly, *c.* 1904. Notice the dairymen. Clarges Street was built in 1716 on a field belonging to Sir William Pulteney, who had appointed his friend, Sir Thomas Clarges, as his trustee. The Clarges were said to be 'of lowly and dubious origin' before the Restoration which reversed their fortunes and led to the marriage of Anne, 'without either wit or beauty', to the Duke of Albemarle, a hero of the day.

Hertford Street, Mayfair, *c.* 1904. Laid out in the 1760s, the street's name was probably taken from the Hertford Arms, a now vanished inn commemorating Lord Hertford, 'the proud Duke' (1662–1748). Originally a fashionable residential street, largely used for offices today, no. 10 was designed by Robert Adam. Famous former residents include Sheridan, Bulwer-Lytton and Earl Grey.

Ebury Street, Pimlico, *c.* 1910. A nursemaid and her charge walk along this former country track, the road here revealing the mixture of mud and horse manure which used to be a hazard to travellers. Mozart stayed here in 1764 at the age of eight and is said to have written his first symphony during his visit. He performed at the nearby Ranelagh Gardens, which had disappeared by the time the street became built-up in the 1820s.

These two views, taken for a report by the Medical Officer of Health, present a stark contrast to the more fashionable streets, and serve as a reminder that, in Westminster, rich and poor have always existed in close proximity. The demolition of these houses, part of John Johnson's 1820s development, made way for Lutyens's 'chequerboard' flats of the Page Street estate, which opened in 1930. Above are the backs of houses on the west side of Johnson Street. Below the children are standing on the corner of Vincent Street and Kensington Place, 1928.

CHAPTER THREE

SHOPS

*Built up by 1682, Coventry Street was described by Tallis in 1839 as 'entirely composed of retail shops'.
Nos 10 to 12, on the east side of the now-vanished Arundell Street, were demolished in 1920 to make way
for the extension of Lyons' Corner House. Seen here about 1870, it is a good example of a typical early
nineteenth-century shop front, with its continuous band of small-paned display windows. The assistants
standing to attention outside suggest pride in this long-lasting establishment.*

John Harriss, standing at the door of his shop in Green Street (renamed Irving Street in 1938), Leicester Square, *c*. 1870. He is described as a picture dealer in directories of the time, but appears to have sold a bizarre range of objects, as the plaque 'The Old Curiosity Shop' implies. A former occupant of the house was William Woollett (1735–85) the engraver. The shop was demolished in 1897.

The Spiking family outside their baker's shop at 5 Dover Street, 9 January 1903. The delivery carts are waiting outside to take the loaves round the streets.

Swan and Edgar's, 1898. Established in 1812, this is one of the earliest surviving high-class retailers who made their home in Regent Street. Little is known about George Swan, who died in 1821. His partner, William Edgar, was the son of a Cumberland farmer who started his London career by selling men's haberdashery on a market stall. The Georgian building at Piccadilly Circus was rebuilt between 1924 and 1928. The notice in the middle is a reminder that Swan and Edgar's did not yet own the entire site, but they were soon to take over Alleyne and Co. next door.

Hamleys, 1898. This view of the premises of another well-known name in Regent Street shows the original look of the street before it was rebuilt on a grander scale in the 1920s. Designed by Nash, the street was completed in 1820 and immediately became a fashionable shopping area.

These shops in the Haymarket in 1898 could be mistaken for Paris not London. Maison Nicol is advertising coils of hair for sale. This reflects women's fashions of the day: real hair was combed back over a pad of false hair and gathered into a loose chignon at the back. More complicated arrangements were used for evening wear, frequently using false hair to supplement one's own. The prices suggest that only the wealthy would shop here.

Joseph Box, court bootmaker, opened his shop in Regent Street in 1834. Nash's attractive Georgian façade, which disappeared in the 1920s, can be seen here about 1910. The firm later moved to Grosvenor Street, and was taken over by John Lobb's in 1956.

This unusual view shows the interior of Joseph Box's shop. Taken in about 1910 it shows the ladies' boots, with their rows of tiny buttons, which were then in fashion.

The toy and shawl department of Liberty, Regent Street, *c.* 1920. In the decoration of the interior, as well as the goods for sale, evidence can be seen of the aesthetic movement which was the inspiration behind the store. Founded by Arthur Liberty in 1875 as East India House, it promoted a fashion for soft draping oriental silks. Liberty's distinctive style is known today all over the world.

Long Acre (the name signifying it was originally a strip in a larger open field) was laid out about 1615. Coaches began to be built here in the mid-seventeenth century when they first became popular and by the beginning of the nineteenth century almost all the premises in the street were involved in the coachmaking industry. In these two photographs, both taken in 1903, we see Long Acre at a time of transition. Carriages continued to be sold here until about 1916, but already they were being supplanted by the motor car. Fiat, Daimler and Mercedes all had premises here in the twentieth century.

The British Automobile Syndicate replaced the coachmaking firm of Henry J. Hall and Sons, at 97–98 Long Acre, in 1902. Joseph Kempster (above) continued to build coaches at 39 Long Acre until 1911 when the premises were taken over by the Piccadilly Motor and Aeroplane Company.

Taken in the days before ordinary people had their own transport, these photographs are a reminder that many shops made home deliveries. Harry Jenks had his 'Grocery, Oil and Italian Stores' on the corner of Tachbrook Street and Charlwood Street – oil was a particular household necessity for lighting. Jenks is seen here in 1903, when horses were still used almost without exception for commercial traffic.

Twining's is probably the oldest shop in Westminster to remain in continuous occupation of the same site. Thomas Twining, supplier of tea to Queen Anne, established his business at 216 Strand in 1706. This magnificent van was built at French's motor engineering works in about 1920.

Villiers Street was built on the site of York House in 1670 but most of the west side was demolished for Charing Cross station in the 1860s. This photograph of no. 34 was taken in 1906, when Challice, the chemist, was advertising 'instant relief' for 'hoemorrhoids'. Patent medicines, often by quack doctors, were commonly resorted to before medically proven remedies became available.

Macclesfield Street was originally built in 1685. This four-storey house of plain brick at no. 9 was rebuilt in 1729 as an optician's shop. The handsome wooden shop front, probably made of deal, had bays divided by Ionic columns in the Palladian style. This photograph was taken in 1883 shortly before it was demolished to make way for Shaftesbury Avenue.

John Bailey (1848–1917), a sanitary engineer who had nine children, is seen here outside his shop, 13 Bateman Street, Soho, *c.* 1910. His first shop was at 20 Meard Street but he had moved here by 1906.

Bryant & Velvin, butcher's shop, 24 Bedfordbury, *c.* 1925. The shop was owned by Robert Lapthorn Velvin (b. 1873), seen here in the bowler hat. In the striped apron is his son Robert William Lapthorn Velvin (b. 1906), who was a choir boy at St Martin-in-the-Fields.

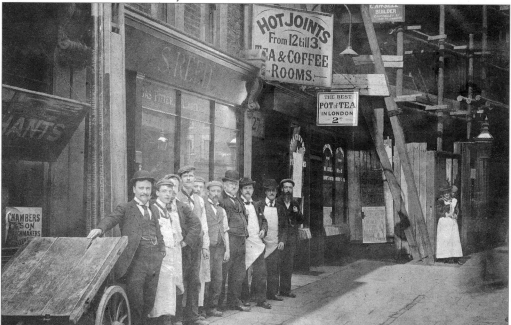

There were many small shops in Foubert's Place, Soho where this staff group is pictured outside the builder's shop of Samuel Reed at no. 25 in about 1894. Reed can be seen in the centre, wearing a bowler hat. On the far left is his son Clarence, next to younger brother Benjamin. A third son, Sidney, is to the right of his father. The shop to the left is Pearson and Co., glass merchants, while to the right hot joints could be purchased at George West's coffee rooms.

A visitor to St James's Park in 1765 wrote, 'The cows are driven about noon and evening to the gate which leads from the Park to the quarter of Whitehall'. Their milk could then be bought 'in little mugs at the rate of 1*d* per mug'. By the early years of the twentieth century when this photograph was taken, there was only one cow at St James's Park but it was still possible to buy milk there.

Market Street, Mayfair, *c.* 1916. This local shopping centre was part of Shepherd Market, founded by Edward Shepherd in 1735 'for the buying and selling of flesh, fish, fowl, roots, herbs and other provisions for human food'. The land had been used from 1686 to hold the notorious annual May Fair but by the early eighteenth century it had become a byword for riotous and disorderly behaviour.

J.B. Thomas, fruitbroker, Covent Garden, *c.* 1920. London's best-known fruit and vegetable market began as early as 1654 with a few market stalls but really became established in 1670 when the Earl of Bedford was granted a licence to hold a market every day except Sunday and Christmas Day. It remained there until 1973, when the market moved to Battersea.

In 1858, Frederick Gorringe opened a single shop in Buckingham Palace Road for the sale of dry goods. He built up a prosperous business, gradually bought up the leases of the adjoining shops and opened other departments. The hosiery department is seen here in the 1930s. It had earlier been a favourite place to shop for the ladies of Queen Victoria's household at Buckingham Palace. Gorringe's closed in the 1960s.

CHAPTER FOUR

HEALTH AND EDUCATION

Grey Coat boy, John Richards, c. 1872. Before the nineteenth century education for the poor was provided by charity schools, of which a number were founded in Westminster during the seventeenth and eighteenth centuries, taking their names from the colour of the uniforms the children were required to wear. The Grey Coat Hospital was founded in 1698 by a group of local shopkeepers who were appalled by the inability of parish nurses employed to look after orphaned and neglected children to keep them off the streets. In 1701 the school moved into the parish workhouse; it remains in the same building today.

In 1874, The Grey Coat Hospital became a day school for girls, the boys being transferred to the United Westminster School in Palace Street. Elsie Day was Headmistress from 1874 to 1910. Her god-daughter is seen here in about 1890; the costume was worn from 1701 and not abandoned until 1875. Underclothes, consisting of home-made stays and black serge petticoats, descended from child to child, unwashed, until they wore out.

By 1936 The Grey Coat Hospital had raised £600 to endow a cot at Westminster Hospital as well as paying £30 a year for its maintenance. Support also took the form of an annual 'Pound Day' when children gave food to Westminster Hospital in 1 lb parcels. This photograph, taken in 1938, includes some small boys. Two forms of boys aged between five and seven closed when war broke out the following year.

Grey Coat girls gardening before evacuation to Brighton in 1939. In 1940, after the fall of France, the evacuees were moved to Farnham. The school returned to Westminster in 1943.

A gymnasium was built at The Grey Coat Hospital in 1882, although there was no apparatus for some years. In 1900 gym was introduced as an optional subject. This gym class (1911) shows girls wearing the two types of costume that were allowed at the time and which included knee-length serge bloomers. All girls wore black woollen stockings and black plimsolls in the gym. For rope climbing and vaulting, the top of the skirt could be tucked into the bloomers, provided it was dropped back into place immediately.

Massed drill for pupils in the playground of the Burdett Coutts and Townshend Foundation Schools, c. 1916. After the 1870 Education Act made primary education compulsory for all, many church schools were founded in Westminster. This school, in Rochester Street, was founded in 1876 under the endowment of the Revd Chauncey Hare Townshend and is known today simply as Burdett Coutts School, after Baroness Burdett-Coutts who was an early trustee and supporter.

Opportunities for girls who attended elementary schools were limited. Most were expected to become servants or dressmakers, and the curriculum was designed to provide them with a basic domestic training. These girls at the Burdett Coutts and Townshend Foundation Schools are having a laundry class in about 1916. They are using flat irons, which can be seen with their stands.

This photograph showing boys having a cookery class at the Burdett Coutts and Townshend Foundation Schools in about 1916 is an unusual example of equal opportunities at this time.

These infants at the Burdett Coutts and Townshend Foundation Schools are having a knitting lesson in about 1916. Notice the slates in front of them. Judging from the shape of the room there may have been another class being taught at the same time on the opposite side; this was not unusual.

Mending day at the Burdett Coutts and Townshend Foundation Schools, *c.* 1916. At many elementary schools girls would spend every afternoon sewing, while the boys did arithmetic. The clothes would sometimes be sold to raise money for the school.

A class at St Michael's Boys School, Ebury Square, Pimlico, 1896. St Michael's schools (strictly segregated into boys, girls and infants) were founded in 1848, the first to be built in the new district of Pimlico. Until then the more prosperous residents sent their children to private schools elsewhere while no provision was made for the rest. The teachers are Mr Battle and Miss Chalk. Gilbert H. Duguid, aged eleven, is sixth from the left in the third row; he is one of several boys wearing sailor suits, which were very popular.

A class at St Michael's Girls School, Ebury Square, Pimlico, 1894. Thomas Cubitt was so concerned that the school would lower the tone of the area, that the school was built on the edge of his development, backing on to the canal. The entrance was on the canal side so that local residents would not be subjected to the noise of the children. After the coming of the railway in 1860, the school moved to new premises.

Benjamin Cunningham is one of the ten year olds seen here in Class 4 at Millbank School, Erasmus Street, in 1910. The school opened in the 1890s on the new Millbank housing estate built on the site of the Millbank Penitentiary.

Westminster School, c. 1910. The only long-established London school to remain on its original site, Westminster School has been teaching scholars in the precincts of the Abbey since at least 1394, offering a classical education for those destined for the professions. It continues to be one of the country's foremost public schools. Front row, left to right: Revd Nall, Mr J. Sargeaunt, Mr Tanner, Revd J. Gow, Mr Fox, Revd Raynor, Mr Huckwell. Second row: Mr Etheridge, Mr Tyson, Mr Day, Mr Hardy, Mr Wootton, Mr Orr, Mr Michell, Mr Smedley. Back Row: Mr Liddell, Mr Burrell, Mr Reed.

Westminster Cathedral group with Monsignor Brown, 1914. The ladies may have been linked to Westminster Cathedral School, which was founded after the building of the Cathedral in 1903.

The first free public library in London to be established under the Public Libraries Act, opened in Great Smith Street, Westminster, on 10 March 1857. This photograph was taken in 1894 just before the library moved to a new building almost opposite the original site. In 1996 the library moved to Victoria Street to cater for the changing needs of a commuter rather than residential population.

Mayfair and Victoria libraries were designed by Arthur Bolton and opened in 1894/5, on land given rent free by the Duke of Westminster. This is the original newspaper and magazine room at Victoria library in Buckingham Palace Road and is now part of the busy lending library.

Library users did not originally have open access to books as it was thought this would encourage heavy losses by theft. This view shows the library indicator at Buckingham Palace Road Library in about 1910. A reader had to find a book he or she wanted in the catalogue, and then check the number against the entry on the indicator. If the number was on a red background, the book was already on loan; if it was on a blue background, it was available and the staff would produce it.

A further development of the library service in Westminster was the provision of a Home Library Service in 1947 to bring books to house-bound readers. This reader has just received a delivery at the Peabody Buildings, Vauxhall Bridge Road, shortly after the service began. Notice the old radio with headphones.

Emanuel Hospital, James Street, was one of a number of almshouses in Westminster founded by private individuals for the benefit of the aged poor. In 1602 four acres on the edge of Tothill Fields, now the site of the St James's Hotel, Buckingham Gate, were purchased under the will of Lady Anne Dacre. There was provision for ten men and ten women, who were all required to attend daily service in the Hospital chapel. This photograph, with Miss Woolmer sketching in the foreground, was taken in 1887 shortly before the buildings were demolished.

St George's Union Workhouse, Fulham Road, opened in 1878. In 1913 it became the City of Westminster Union Workhouse, housing the sick and aged poor from all Westminster parishes. At one time it contained 808 inmates, the largest number of any infirmary in London and is seen here in 1919. In 1925 the name was changed to St Stephen's Hospital, to try to remove the fear of the workhouse.

The City of Westminster Workhouse, Fulham Road, is seen here bedecked for Peace Celebration Day, 19 July 1919, to mark the signing of the peace treaty at the end of the First World War. Margaret Ainsworth, whose niece donated this picture to Westminster Archives, was head of the receiving ward at this date. Before free health care, the old and infirm were often forced into the workhouse, a prospect which filled many with dread. The rows of old women on hard wooden benches (below) are a bleak sight, despite the festive decorations.

The Infants' Hospital, Vincent Square, 1908. Founded by Robert Mond and Ralph Vincent in a small house in Hampstead in 1903, the hospital moved to Vincent Square in 1906. As well as treating children, the hospital trained doctors and nurses, and furthered research into infant mortality. Run by voluntary contributions, it was in constant need of funding. In 1947 it became the Westminster Children's Hospital.

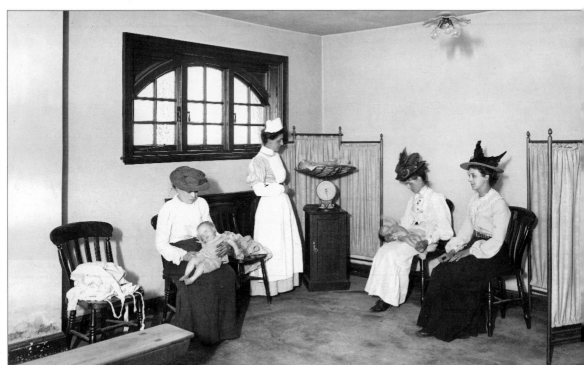

An important aim of the Infants' Hospital was to teach women to be good mothers. The mother and baby clinic is seen here in 1908.

Westminster Hospital was the first in London to be founded by voluntary contributions; it began in 1715 when four gentlemen founded a society to assist the 'industrious sick and needy'. The site for the hospital, seen here in 1921, in Broad Sanctuary, opposite Westminster Abbey, was bought in 1831 and opened for patients in 1834. It was built by William and Charles Inwood at a cost of £40,000. The hospital remained here until 1939, when it moved to a new building in St John's Gardens, Horseferry Road. The building in Broad Sanctuary was demolished in 1951 and replaced by the Queen Elizabeth II Centre.

This animal hospital, known as 'Our Dumb Friends' League', was first listed at no. 1 Hugh Street, Belgrave Road in 1908, with Arthur Coke as its secretary. Seen here in about 1920, it was incorporated into the Blue Cross Hospital in about 1957 but has continued at the same address, which is currently the Blue Cross's headquarters.

St James's Park Open-Air School was set up to restore children to health and strength through fresh air, rest, exercise and nourishing food. Tuberculosis and malnutrition were rife in the early years of the twentieth century when thousands of sick children were unable to attend school. The open-air system flourished for a number of years, until overtaken by modern medicine and improved living standards. Blankets and hot milk are being used here in November 1934 to relieve the spartan conditions of the open-sided classroom.

Rest was important to restore health and a rest period was allocated every day from 1 to 2 p.m. The beds in use here in 1934 were later replaced by tubular steel ones.

CHAPTER FIVE

TRANSPORT

This peaceful view of the Thames, looking across to Waterloo Bridge, is a reminder that the river was the major thoroughfare from Roman times until the late eighteenth century, when thousands of watermen who made their living from rowing passengers across the Thames were made redundant by the new bridges. The Waterloo Bridge, seen here about 1880, was built in 1811 but began to crumble in 1923. A battle raged in the 1930s over its rebuilding and it was finally replaced by the present bridge during the Second World War.

Westminster Bridge was the second to be built across the Thames after London Bridge. Opened in 1750, the stone bridge ran into problems almost from the first when its piers began to settle into the river bed. In 1862 it was replaced by a cast-iron bridge built by Thomas Page. Both were tremendous feats of engineering. This view, showing traffic on the bridge in about 1890, looks across towards St Thomas's Hospital.

Vauxhall Bridge was London's first iron bridge across the Thames and opened in 1816. It was replaced between 1895 and1906 by the present bridge designed by Sir Alexander Binnie. Here is one of the cast iron arches of the new bridge under construction in the late 1890s.

The decline of the paddle-steamers, which had their heyday in the 1840s, was blamed on the *Princess Alice* disaster in 1878 when a pleasure boat carrying 700 passengers capsized with great loss of life; the arrival of the railways and omnibuses was probably more to blame. In 1905 London County Council introduced its river steamboat service, seen here in about 1908. The boats were named after famous people who had associations with the river.

Originally constructed by the Chelsea Waterworks Company in 1725 to supply drinking water from the Thames, the Grosvenor Canal was enlarged in the 1820s, when the Grosvenor Estate realized its commercial potential. The canal was used to transport materials for the building of Belgravia and Pimlico, but also provided a pleasant outlook for the mansions along its banks. The lock-keeper is seen here in about 1900.

The Grosvenor Canal ran behind Buckingham Palace Road, and wharves still lined the southern part of the road in the early twentieth century. Labourers, seen here in 1928, are engaged on the reconstruction of the Grosvenor canal lock and basin.

The opening of the new Grosvenor canal lock and basin took place on 3 July 1929. Here the Mayor of Westminster, Major Vivian Rogers, can be seen laying a stone to mark the event.

Railway companies had been looking for a site for a station north of the Thames for some time when cholera epidemics led to the Act of 1852 preventing drinking water being taken out of the Thames. The redundant basin of the Grosvenor Canal made an ideal site for Victoria station, which opened in 1860. The changes in transport during the early part of the twentieth century are clearly illustrated in these two postcards. The same print has been retouched (below), replacing the horse-drawn cabs with motor cars, and the horse-drawn omnibus with a motor bus. These changes happened between 1910 and 1914.

The hansom cab, seen here about 1895, was introduced in the 1830s and reached its peak in the 1890s. In 1898 there were 11,547 horse cabs in London. The first motor cabs appeared in 1903 and by 1910 were in the ascendancy. The last horse cabs were licensed in 1943 and had disappeared from the streets by 1947.

Once the motor car replaced the carriage among Westminster's wealthier residents, redundant coachmen found new employment as chauffeurs, and stables became garages. There were no driving tests until 1935. The chauffeur here is Albert Crisp, in Eaton Mews South, *c.* 1913.

Parking was as much a problem for horse owners in the nineteenth century as it is for car owners in London in the late twentieth. Many preferred to hire a horse and carriage when needed from a job master. Patrick Hearn, described as a job and carriage master, advertised 'contracts for any period, horses and carriages for yearly or other jobs'. He owned a number of yards including this one at Lemon Tree Yard, Bedfordbury, photographed on 3 June 1898.

Staff on an outing from Short's wine merchants are seen here outside their premises in the Strand, *c.* 1918. It was a long-established business, first set up in 1726.

Annual outing of staff from Bishop's, Elizabeth Street, Pimlico, 1875. The founder of the firm, Joseph James Bishop (1834–99) is on the box. He came from Norfolk as a young man and in 1854 opened a greengrocer's shop at 23 Elizabeth Street, Pimlico. Needing a delivery cart for his fruit, he soon saw the possibilities of launching out into furniture removals, especially as he was so close to Victoria station.

This horse-drawn pantechnicon and trailer were in use in the late nineteenth century until replaced by motor traction. Joseph James Bishop had three sons who had all been taken into partnership by 1878 when the name of his furniture removals business was changed accordingly. In 1872 he acquired a warehouse in Hugh Street and in 1875 another in Ebury Street.

In 1927 Bishop & Sons became a limited company and acquired 10 and 12 Belgrave Road as warehouse premises. The firm continued to expand, transporting furniture all over the world, and is still in existence today after more than 140 years. This shows some of the twenteith-century developments in their fleet of motorized vehicles.

The history of the London bus begins in 1829 when George Shillibeer introduced his horse-drawn service from Paddington to the Bank along Marylebone Road. The London General Omnibus Company was formed in 1856 and by the end of the nineteenth century omnibuses were passing along major roads – such as the Strand seen here in the 1890s – at the rate of three or four a minute in each direction. The crews worked far longer hours than the horses. A two-horse omnibus needed eleven or twelve horses to keep it on the road all day.

Motor buses were first introduced in 1910 and the horse bus disappeared with great speed. All horse buses were withdrawn in August 1914 at the outbreak of the First World War because the Army needed the horses. A policeman is seen here directing the traffic in the Strand about 1925.

Livestock was once a common sight in London's streets as it was driven to butchers and meat markets to be slaughtered. These sheep, seen in the Strand in 1924, make an incongruous picture with the motorized buses.

The first of the double-decker buses with covered tops can be seen in this view of the Strand. They were introduced in 1926.

The first underground train ran in 1862. The Central London Railway opened in 1900, including Oxford Circus station seen here at about that time. The company decided to have a flat rate fare of *2d* for any journey, which earned it the nickname of 'The Twopenny Tube'.

Steam buses were first tried in 1902 but withdrawn after two months. Later trials had a little more success. A small number of Thomas Clarkson's National Steam Car Company buses were introduced in 1909 and did well during the First World War, but were withdrawn in 1919.

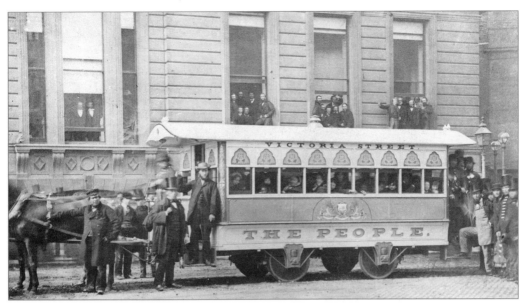

In 1861 an American, George Francis Train, laid a single line of rail from Westminster Abbey along Victoria Street. His experimental tram, based on a prototype from his native Philadelphia, was not a success. A register of accidents caused by the tram rails, which were raised above the surface, records the hazard it presented to other horse traffic. It was another ten years before horse trams became accepted in London.

This is a rare view of the Grantham steam tramcar, tried in Vauxhall Bridge Road in November 1873. Horse transport was very expensive and several attempts were made to replace it by steam but although successfully used on the railways, it ultimately proved too heavy for the roads.

Although trams were in use from the 1870s, the Cities of London and Westminster continued to ban them from operating within their boundaries. It was not until the opening of the Kingsway tram subway in 1908 that a through-route was established, by which time single-deck electric cars were in use, as seen here on the Embankment. The tunnel was rebuilt to take double-deckers in 1930/31. The subway closed in 1952 and part of it was converted into the Strand underpass, which opened to road traffic in 1964.

This tram, seen on 16 July 1950, was diverted via Blackfriars during the construction of the Festival of Britain footbridge at Charing Cross. It is entering the Kingsway subway at Waterloo Bridge on the wrong track. Note the pointsman's hut on the left.

A tram stops at Westminster during the Saturday midday peak, 18 November 1950. For southbound passengers at Blackfriars there was a shelter in John Carpenter Street and a larger shelter nearer the bridge, the latter used by all trams in the slack hour. A third shelter on the riverside at Blackfriars was similar to that at Westminster seen here.

Trams disappeared from the London streets on 5 July 1952. Here on 10 May 1952 a tram passes the RAF Memorial on the Victoria Embankment between Westminster and Charing Cross bridges. The trees still bear white black-out rings, which were painted on during the war. In the background is the Bailey footbridge to the Festival of Britain site.

The Westminster paving scandal was responsible for this view of Great George Street in 1905, showing pools of water on blocks of red gum. Road maintenance was a real problem because the wheels of omnibuses sank into a macadam surface. Wood paving was a more durable alternative and used extensively in Westminster. But in 1901 an American, Edward Alcott, sold the council substandard blocks of red gum, with the results seen above. Another hazard of wood paving was that when it rained, a film of liquid dung made it slippery for horses.

Taxis waiting by the side entrance of Victoria station, Buckingham Palace Road in 1924.

CHAPTER SIX

AT WORK

Flower-women were a colourful feature of London and are seen here outside St Paul's, Covent Garden, about 1880. A flower-sellers' memorial window in St Clement Danes preserves the memory of Fanny, one of the best-known and last of the flower girls, who died in 1923.

Women shelling peas at Covent Garden, *c*. 1920. They were employed to supply hotels and restaurants. Women also acted as porters, and were renowned for their strength. A newspaper account of 1840 records how the friends of an inebriated tailor employed one of the market women to carry him home.

Boys employed as casual labour at Covent Garden, *c*. 1915. The building seen here dates from 1830, although the cast-iron roof was not added until 1875. The market moved out in 1973 and the area has been tastefully restored as shops and restaurants.

Porters at Covent Garden, *c.* 1930. These men may have been practising for the annual basket-carrying competition which used to be held at the market.

Westminster City Council took over the running of public services in 1900. Street cleaning was a major task and the depot at Gatliff Road was a very busy one. Once refuse had been collected from the streets it was taken away by barge down the Grosvenor Canal. These two views were taken in about 1903 outside the office at Gatliff Road. One of the street-cleaning carts can be seen above, while below is a staff group.

Spruce paving being laid on the east side of Trafalgar Square, looking towards Northumberland Avenue, August 1904. Wood blocks were used for many road surfaces in Westminster at the beginning of the twentieth century. Wealthier residents preferred wood to macadam because it muffled the noise of the traffic but drivers complained that the surface became too slippery for the horses when wet.

Street cleaning in Broad Sanctuary, looking towards Westminster Abbey, Middlesex Guildhall and Westminster Hospital, c. 1913.

George Smith and Sons, wholesale furriers, was founded in 1794 in Gough Square. In 1949, when this picture of fur matching for making coats was taken, the firm was at Liberty House in Regent Street. It later moved to Kingly Street and closed in 1988. Surviving company records give an insight into the growth and decline of the fur trade, and the impact of the Second World War on a small firm.

The woollen warehouse of S. Addington and Co., 4–6 Charing Cross Road, 1922. Built in 1892 the warehouse became the home of the Italian Fascist Club in the 1930s. The building is now occupied by Charing Cross Library, which opened in 1948, and the balconies seen here are full of books.

Vacher and Sons, publishers, Great Smith Street, *c.* 1925. Established in Westminster in 1751, the stationers, lithographers and printers business moved to this new building on the corner of Abbey Orchard Street in 1903. The firm remained here until 1957 when it moved to Clerkenwell Road. The compositors can be seen at work below.

Workers at the Stag Brewery, 1922. The name of the brewery was taken from the coat of arms of William Greene who began brewing here in 1641. In 1837 it was bought by James Watney and became the headquarters of Watney's before its demolition in 1959. Today the brewery, which was near Victoria station, is remembered in Stag Place.

A milk woman from William Sim's Dairy, 129 Jermyn Street, 1864. Until the twentieth century cows were kept in cellars in Westminster and milk was bought by the jugful. In the nineteenth and early twentieth centuries many Welsh men and women came to London to set up dairies to meet the need of London's growing population for fresh milk.

Charles Mahillon and Co. musical instrument works, 182 Wardour Street, *c.* 1910. The firm, which manufactured 'orchestral, military and contesting band instruments on scientific principles', began in Leicester Square in 1884, moving to Oxford Street three years later, and then to Wardour Street in 1891. It closed in 1922.

Krieger Electric Carriage Syndicate, 48a Gillingham Street, Eccleston Square, Pimlico, *c.* 1908. The manufacture of electric cars was shortlived, this firm being in existence from 1903 to 1918. The premises were then used for another new invention – the manufacture of aircraft wings.

Westminster Fire Station, Greycoat Place, opened on 22 May 1906, replacing the old fire station in Francis Street. Firemen are seen here with the hand hose cart in 1907.

The stables at Knightsbridge Fire Station, Relton Mews, Montpelier Square, *c.* 1912. Until the Metropolitan Fire Brigade was set up in 1866, the parish fire engines often competed with each other. Those who had horse power, rather than manpower, usually won.

One of the commissionaires at Scott's restaurant, *c.* 1910. The restaurant in Coventry Street was opened by the proprietors of the London Pavilion Music-Hall in 1872 as an 'oyster warehouse'. It became known as Scott's Oyster and Supper Rooms in 1891 and for the next fifty years was one of the best-known fish restaurants in Europe. It moved to Mount Street, Mayfair, in 1967.

Kitchen staff at the Hotel Victoria, Northumberland Avenue, 1897. Despite these impressive kitchens, there were only four bathrooms for its 500 guests. Built to the designs of Isaacs and Florence between 1882 and 1885, it is now Northumberland House.

The courtyard of the Savoy Hotel, Strand, 1892. Designed by T.E. Collcutt, the hotel opened in 1889, next to the Savoy Theatre. It was one of the earliest hotels in London to provide a high ratio of bathrooms to bedrooms and to be fitted with electric lifts and lights. It was remodelled in 1910.

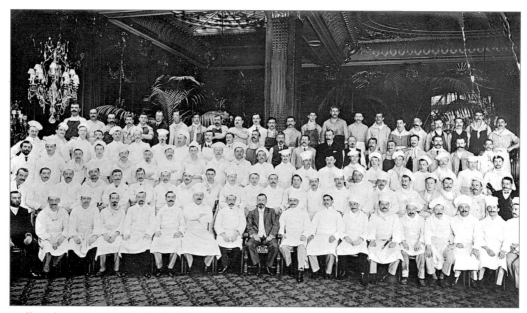

Staff at the opening of the Piccadilly Hotel, 1908. Designed by Norman Shaw, this hotel with 294 bedrooms was built between 1905 and 1908 on the site of St James's Hall.

Pinoli's restaurant, 17 Wardour Street, *c.* 1910. Charles Pinoli was renowned for his wines, as this view of the cellars suggests. His restaurant was advertised as giving the 'Best 2/- dinner in London'.

CHAPTER SEVEN

LEISURE

Café de Paris dancer, 1925. The mirror-covered walls, copied from the ballroom of RMS Titanic, *made this a well-known nightclub in the 1920s and '30s. Located in the converted basement of the Rialto Cinema, in Coventry Street, it was thought to be a safe place during the Blitz but received a direct hit in 1941 when a large number of customers and the bandleader were killed.*

St Gabriel's Company of the London Diocesan Church Lads' Brigade, associated with St Gabriel's School, Pimlico, during annual camp at The Redoubt, Eastbourne, *c.* 1908. The bearded figure in the centre is Captain B.H. Springett, who lived in Winchester Street. The two boys on the left of the back row are the Goodall brothers.

Officers and men of the Civil Service (12th Middlesex) Rifle Volunteers, *c.* 1883. During the First World War they served with the Kensington volunteers in Palestine. Volunteer groups were first raised in Westminster in 1793 to resist the threat of invasion by Napoleon Bonaparte.

City of Westminster Football Club, 1908/9.

Westminster City Council staff who competed in the Inter Metropolitan Borough Officers Walking Race, 10 October 1903. The shield was presented by the City of Westminster.

Boys paddling in the Serpentine, Hyde Park, 1906. George Lansbury (1859–1940) is remembered for ordering the building of the first public bathing place on the shore of the Serpentine, but it was popular from the early nineteenth century. In June 1837 William Tayler recorded in his diary that about 1,500 men and boys bathed in the Serpentine on a Sunday morning, although they had to get out of the water by 8.00 a.m.

Rowing on the Serpentine, Hyde Park, c. 1908. The Serpentine was formed in 1730 at the instigation of Queen Caroline by damming the Westbourne, then a muddy stream, and transforming it into a spectacular lake. It has been the focus for leisure activities ever since.

St George's Baths, Buckingham Palace Road, *c*. 1900. The parish of St George Hanover Square opened the first baths on this site in 1856 when Wallace Ramage was employed as 'the teacher of swimming'. The baths were rebuilt in the 1880s, the Italianate, pedimented design seen here being the work of F. J. Smith. Winston Churchill was among those who learnt to swim here. Described in 1950 as 'the leading public swimming bath in the Metropolis', it was demolished in 1972.

The architecture of the new baths was on a grand scale, as seen in this view of a swimming lesson for boys from Burdett Coutts and Townshend Foundation Schools, *c*. 1916.

J.L. Toole (1832–1906) as Toole and Ellen Farren (d. 1904) as Polly in *Seeing Toole*, *c.* 1873. These two much-loved artists of the Victorian stage had a particular comic talent and many of the burlesques performed at the Gaiety in the 1870s were written especially for them. Toole went on to manage his own theatre in King William Street known as the Folly Theatre.

Her Majesty's Theatre, on the corner of Haymarket and Pall Mall, *c.* 1860. Opened in 1791, this was the second theatre on the site and the largest in England. Remodelled in 1816, Nash's arcade can be seen here. During the golden years of 1830 to 1850, when Jenny Lind made her debut here, the theatre was known as the Italian Opera House. Destroyed by fire in 1867, the present theatre (the fourth) dates from 1897.

London Hippodrome, Cranbourn Street, 1902. Opened in 1900 as a combined music-hall and circus with a built-in water tank, its water shows made theatrical history in the opening decade of the twentieth century. After reconstruction in 1912, it became the venue for successful revues and variety shows, and in 1958 was altered again to become The Talk of the Town, a cabaret and restaurant which closed in 1982.

P. Bury and Edward Marshall as the Gendarmes in *Genevieve de Brabant* at the Gaiety Theatre, 1872. The Gaiety, which opened in 1868, was one of a number of theatres in a maze of narrow streets behind the eastern end of the Strand. Under John Hollingshead it specialized in burlesque. It was demolished in 1903 to make way for the development of the Aldwych and Kingsway.

The Gaiety Theatre, on the corner of Aldwych and the Strand, 1913. Designed by Norman Shaw and opened in 1903, the new theatre became well known for producing successful musicals with its famous 'Gaiety Girls'. The theatre closed in 1939 and was finally demolished in 1957. The site is now occupied by Citibank House.

Nelly Bromley as Praline and Angelina Claude as Rosalie in *Nemesis* at the Strand Theatre, 1873. This little theatre on the south of the Strand between Surrey Street and Strand Lane opened in 1832 in a building which had begun life in 1803 as a panorama. Rebuilt in 1882, it was demolished in 1905 and is now the site of the Aldwych tube station.

The London Pavilion, Piccadilly Circus, c. 1880. Originally a song-and-supper-room annexe to the Black Horse Inn, it became a music-hall in 1861. The building seen here was demolished in 1885 and replaced by a new Pavilion, the façade of which still stands. In 1918 it became a theatre, and was converted into a cinema in 1934. This closed in 1982 and the building was refurbished to become shops.

The Palace Theatre, Cambridge Circus, 1890. Opened as The Royal English Opera House in 1891, it was built by T.E. Collcutt and G.H. Holloway for Richard D'Oyly Carte, but financial failure soon forced its closure. In 1892 it reopened as the Palace Theatre of Varieties, a music-hall where Anna Pavlova made her London debut in 1910. In 1911 it became the Palace Theatre, but from 1919 to 1923 it was used mainly as a cinema. In 1924 it reopened as a theatre for musicals, for which it is known today.

Sarah Bernhardt (1844–1923) as Princess Lointaine, June 1895. Born in Paris, she was idolized as one of the greatest tragic actresses of her day. After 1876 Bernhardt made frequent appearances in London, appearing at the Gaiety in 1879, Her Majesty's Theatre in 1886, the Lyceum in 1887 and 1889, the Empire in 1892, and the Adelphi in 1897.

The Empire Theatre, Leicester Square, 1917. Crowds are seen here queuing for *Razzle, Dazzle,* a patriotic revue produced by Albert de Courville which opened in 1916. The newsboard is advertising the *Battle of the Somme* at the Scala. The theatre opened in 1881 as the Royal London Panorama, with scenes from the *Charge of the Light Brigade.* In 1884 it reopened as the Empire Theatre, but was not a financial success until its transformation into a music-hall in 1887.

The Empire Cinema, Leicester Square, 1928. The Empire Theatre closed in 1927 when it was demolished and replaced by the Empire Cinema, seen here shortly after its opening. The present cinema on this site dates from 1963.

LONDON COLISEUM
Below the Revolving Stage

The first theatre in England to have a revolving stage, the London Coliseum (renamed the Coliseum Theatre in 1931) opened as a variety house in 1904 designed by Frank Matcham. Seen here in the 1920s, the revolving stage with its three concentric rings, the largest of which was 75 ft in diameter, continued in use until 1955 and was finally removed in the late 1980s.

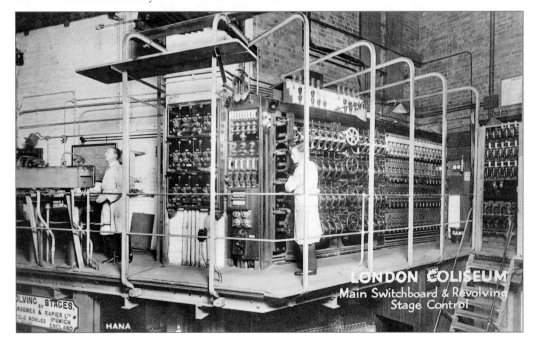

LONDON COLISEUM
Main Switchboard & Revolving
Stage Control

CHAPTER EIGHT

HOUSES AND HOMES

Bathroom in the apartment of Major George Wallace Carpenter at 28 Ashley Place, 1893. This shower is surely well ahead of its time and the tea table adds an intriguing touch to this intimate setting

Old houses in Drury Lane, 1876. A fashionable street in the seventeenth century when Oliver Cromwell and Nell Gwynne lived here, in the eighteenth century it became notorious for its gin shops. The shop seen here on the right was formerly the Cock and Magpie. Many of the old houses were cleared at the end of the nineteenth century to make way for the construction of Kingsway and the Aldwych.

Old houses in Wych Street, 1867. An extension of Drury Lane, this narrow street contained a number of ancient timber-framed houses that overhung the roadway. Wych Street disappeared completely in 1900 when these houses were demolished to make way for the construction of the Aldwych.

The town house of Lord Carrington, 8 Whitehall Yard, 1884. These views offer an unusual glimpse of the inside as well as the outside of one of the grand mansions that sprang up in the eighteenth century on the site of Whitehall Palace (destroyed by fire in 1698). During the nineteenth century, private residents found themselves increasingly surrounded by government offices which infiltrated Whitehall Yard from 1803. The house was demolished in the 1890s to make way for Horseguards Avenue.

The apartment of Major George Wallace Carpenter, at 28 Ashley Place, in 1893. In the late nineteenth century the Victoria Street area became the venue for fashionable mansion flats, particularly for ex-colonials. Oriental styles were very much in vogue, as seen in this opulent boudoir.

By way of contrast a classical influence can be seen here at 2 Eaton Square in 1892. The Victorians had a fascination with the morbid and bizarre, typified by the disembodied hand on the table. It was not uncommon for such models to be cast from the limbs of dead relatives.

Hotel Provence, Leicester Square, *c*. 1892. This terrace on the east side of Leicester Square was built in 1672. Dominique Deneulain opened a boarding house here in 1834 which became the Hotel Provence in 1845 when it was refronted during the widening of Cranbourn Street. The hotel closed in 1913 and the present building on this site dates from 1958 when the rest of the terrace, which suffered bomb damage, was also rebuilt.

A bedroom with wash-stand at the Hotel Cecil, 1896. Declared to be the largest in Europe when it opened in 1886, this hotel in the Strand had over 600 rooms but was later eclipsed by its neighbour, the Savoy. It closed in 1930 and was replaced by Shell Mex House.

The Cottage, 39 Grosvenor Road, Pimlico, in 1908. The family of Sir Kenneth Mackenzie is seen here outside their home which has a typically overgrown Edwardian garden.

Berkeley Arms, 6 John Street, c. 1900. William Sparrow, the innkeeper, is pictured with his family outside their home. Both the inn and the street are named after John Berkeley, a Royalist commander during the Civil War, who in 1642 bought land here which remained in the family for 300 years.

Ashley Gardens, *c.* 1912. The rise of the mansion flat in the 1880s and '90s offered an attractive alternative for those who wanted a central location where they could entertain in style and still have space for servants. Close to Victoria station, this prestigious estate of 227 flats fronting Ambrosden Avenue, Thirleby Road and Emery Hill Street, was built in 1890 next to the site of Tothill Fields Prison where the new Cathedral was in progress.

Millbank Estate, *c.* 1912. The nineteenth century saw great developments in working-class housing, particularly the Peabody Buildings, which culminated in the first London County Council housing estate built on the site of Millbank Prison. The first block, Hogarth, opened in 1899, providing accommodation for 306 people. Rents ranged from 7s to 13s a week and no coppers were provided in the sculleries as residents were expected to take their laundry to the public baths and wash-houses in Great Smith Street.

CHAPTER NINE

WESTMINSTER AT WAR

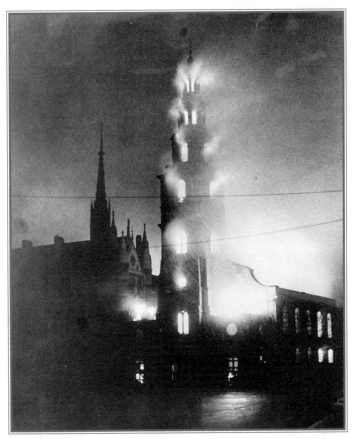

Flames leap from St Clement Danes church in the Strand, May 1941. The original eleventh-century church escaped destruction in the Great Fire of London but its replacement, by Christopher Wren was not so fortunate. The church was bombed in the Blitz, the interior was gutted and the bells were cracked. The steeple and the walls were not too badly damaged and reconstruction was completed in 1958.

Women labourers tar painting in Clarendon Street, May 1918. These unusual views show the impact of the First World War on life in Westminster. The cause of women's suffrage was greatly advanced when women were needed to take over men's jobs.

Women labourers paving in West Halkin Street, December 1918. It is interesting to see that men are supervising the work. Women employed during the First World War were usually on lower rates of pay and had to give up their jobs as soon as the men returned.

Exhibition of war models, 1918. Over £10,000 was raised by Thomas Parsons & Sons in aid of disabled soldiers and sailors through the exhibition of Famous War Models inaugurated by them in their showrooms at 315–317 Oxford Street during the last year of the First World War.

Employment for disabled servicemen between the wars was a major social problem. An exhibition of shoes and boots made by disabled soldiers under a government employment scheme is seen here at the shop of Joseph Box, 45 Conduit Street, in about 1920.

Westminster Civil Defence, *c.* 1939. Based on experiences in the First World War, one of the main worries at the outbreak of the Second World War was the threat of gas attacks. All the men here are carrying gas masks in a bag worn across the front.

The first anti-gas test in London was staged by Westminster City Council in Pimlico on 29 March 1941. Here civil defence personnel can be seen wearing their gas masks and carrying out a casualty.

The first anti-gas test involved the whole community. Here air-raid wardens are helping a casualty. Note the difference between the civilian gas mask, issued to all men, women and children, and the civil defence personnel gas mask worn by the warden on the left.

Wings for Victory week, 6–13 March 1943. As part of a national money-raising effort to finance the war, children were encouraged to buy war savings stamps to stick on this 1,000 lb bomb, with slogans such as 'Knock a nail in Hitler's coffin', and 'Come and plaster the bombs for Berlin'. At the end of the week the bomb was to be dropped on the enemy.

Wings for Victory week, 8 March 1943. To help raise morale, and money, a procession of Allied forces, 'the men whose wings will lead us to victory', marched through London to Trafalgar Square led by the American flag. A Lancaster bomber is on display in the background. London succeeded in raising over £150 million in one week, of which Westminster's target was £10 million.

Demonstration of a mobile kitchen, Hyde Park, 6 October 1942. The WRVS, seen here washing up, played a vital part in providing services to people bombed out of their homes, including providing mobile feeding stations like this one.

Rescuers at work in Great Peter Street following the bombing of the Abbey Printing Works on 11 November 1940, when thirty girls working there were trapped in the debris. St Matthew's Church can be seen behind. The coats still hanging on their pegs are a chilling reminder of how uncertain life was during the war for so many people.

A German plane shot down near Victoria Station, 15 September 1940. Firemen are trying to put out a fire caused by the crash of a Dornier brought down during a bombing raid. The German pilot was killed but a British pilot who crashed at the same time near Ebury Bridge survived. In the wreckage can be seen the engine and part of the fuselage; the rest of the bomber came down on a rooftop a quarter of a mile away.

Gloucester House, Park Lane, 19 April 1941. This block of luxury flats, formerly occupied by millionaires and celebrities, was requisitioned by Westminster City Council to provide shelter for 300 bombed-out and homeless people. Empty mansions in Mayfair and Belgravia were also used as hostels. Some of the homeless, seen here in the lounge, must have found their new surroundings a little daunting.

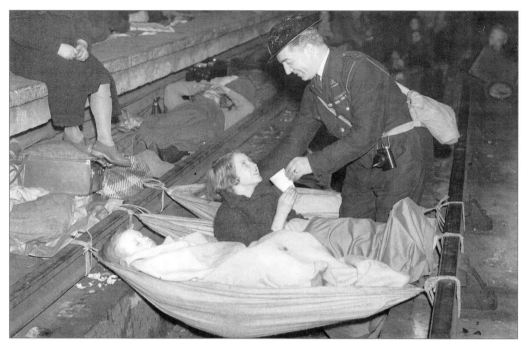

Children sleeping in the tube, 1940. When the Blitz began there was an urgent need for sleeping accommodation because people had to spend whole nights in the shelters which had been designed for sitting or standing room only. In October 1940 it was decided to close the line between Holborn and Aldwych and use the tunnel at Aldwych station as a public shelter for 1,300 people.

Aldwych tube shelter, 1940. At first people slept everywhere, including in the 'suicide pit' alongside the electric rail itself. Later, a wooden floor was made, and bunks erected on the platform. Tickets had to be issued to prevent overcrowding.

CHAPTER TEN

SPECIAL EVENTS

Sir Colin Campbell (1792–1863), hero of the Indian Mutiny, who lived in Berkeley Square, was one of many who have been paid the honour of being buried at Westminster Abbey. This early carte de visite *was taken in Paris by its inventor, Disdéri. Introduced to London in 1858, photography was brought within reach of ordinary families for the first time. The face of the West End was changed, with photographic studios springing up in Regent Street and its surrounding area, and even giving their name to Glasshouse Street, near Piccadilly Circus.*

The start of the procession from Buckingham Palace for Queen Victoria's golden jubilee, June 1887. The whole of the country was involved in the celebrations, which were to be repeated ten years later on the occasion of her diamond jubilee.

Victoria station, dressed for Royalty, November 1901. Crowds are awaiting the arrival of the Duke and Duchess of Cornwall and York on their return from a tour of the Empire shortly after Queen Victoria's death.

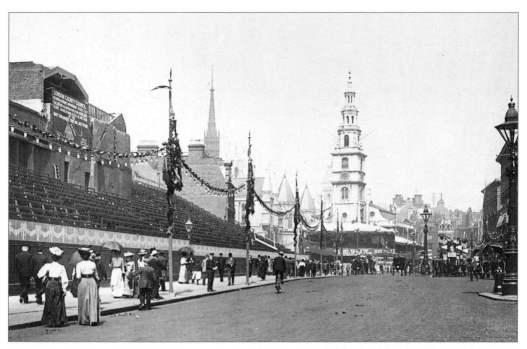

Coronation of Edward VII, 1902. Here can be seen the decorations along the Strand with banks of seating to the left.

Opening of the Italian roof-garden in Duke Street, Mayfair, 1905. This eighteenth-century street was rebuilt between 1886 and 1896, but one of the most notable buildings appeared a little later. C. Stanley Peach's imposing electricity sub-station was completed in 1905. Lord Cheylesmore, Mayor of Westminster (1904–6), is seen here opening the new garden which was ingeniously created on its roof.

THE NELSON CENTENARY.

*The Nelson Celebration
in Trafalgar Square,
London, October 21st, 1905.*

Nelson Centenary Celebrations in Trafalgar Square, 21 October 1905. It was estimated that about 80,000 people flocked to Trafalgar Square for a special service to mark the occasion. One eyewitness recorded, 'there was a great fuss over Nelson . . . wreathes from all over the world – Natal sent a green laurel harp-shape with red ribbon, Cape Town a wreath of white and mauve everlastings and Australia a very large green oval wreath and white chrysanthemums'.

'Woolwich Arsenal demands a fair share of the Nation's Work', 18 May 1907. Trafalgar Square has provided a focus for demonstrations since it was first laid out in 1835. The Chartists began their march here in 1848 and it has since become a popular finishing point for protest marches, as seen here. The Woolwich Arsenal began arms manufacture in Tudor times. Two world wars were to provide more than its fair share of the work demanded here, with up to 40,000 workers employed during the Second World War.

Royal visit, c. 1908. The scene here in Regent Street shows the kind of crowds that still gather today to watch royalty passing by. Notice the spectators on top of the omnibus raising their hats, and the carts waiting in Viga Street. The occasion may have been the visit of the King and Queen of Sweden when a seating platform was set up at Oxford Circus.

Suffragette demonstration in St James Street, 19 June 1910. Members of the Women's Social and Political
Union, known as suffragettes, mounted a vigorous campaign for votes for women in the early years of the
century with street parades, demonstrations and rallies in Hyde Park and Trafalgar Square. The banner
proclaims 'Hope is Strong', but it was not until the end of the First World War that women over thirty
gained the vote, and younger women had to wait until 1928.

Visit of the Australian Prime Minister William Morris Hughes (1864–1952) to the Burdett Coutts and
Townshend Foundation Schools, Rochester Street, 21 March 1916. Born in Wales, Hughes was a former
pupil of the school. He went to Australia in 1884 and became Prime Minister in 1915. An ardent
supporter of the Commonwealth, he is seen here during a trip to London to be made Privy Councillor.

Funeral procession of Nurse Edith Cavell (1865–1915) leaving Victoria station, 15 May 1919. Executed by the Germans for helping Belgian and Allied fugitives, she was heralded as a national heroine and at the end of the First World War her body was brought back for burial in Westminster Abbey. A marble statue of her by Sir George Frampton was erected the following year in St Martin's Place.

Indian Army victory march, 2 August 1919. This was one of several victory parades through the streets of London which marked the end of the First World War. Londoners turned out in force to celebrate, thronging the streets, windows and even rooftops, as seen here.

Beating the Bounds of St Clement Danes Parish, passing through Fountain Court, 25 May 1922. Ascension Day was the traditional time for the priest and people of a parish, led by the beadle, to walk around the parish boundaries. Charity school boys would accompany them and be beaten with willow rods at intervals to help them remember the route. By this date the rods were probably used to beat the buildings rather than the boys.

Mother's Union jubilee service, 22 June 1926. The procession is approaching Westminster Abbey with the diocesan presidents in the foreground.

First meeting of Westminster City Council, 9 November 1900. This captures an historic moment which took place in the former St Martin's Town Hall in Charing Cross Road. Local government was transferred from the parish vestries to a new city council, covering an area which stretched from Knightsbridge in the west to Covent Garden in the east. The present city hall, created when the old borough was joined with Paddington and Marylebone in 1965, is a modern office block in Victoria Street.

Flooding on the night of 6/7 January 1928 caused this scene of devastation in Grosvenor Road, opposite Atterbury Street. When the Thames burst its banks fourteen people were drowned in Westminster basements. The flood drew attention to overcrowding and poor housing in the Page Street area, resulting in its redevelopment.

INDEX

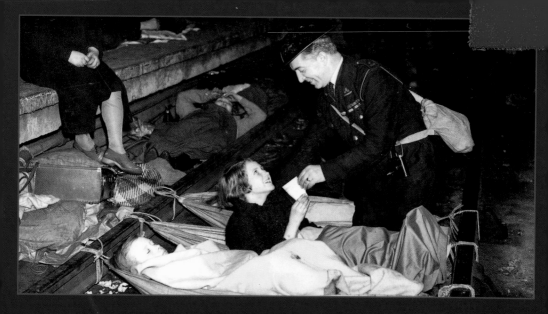

Westminster in Old Photographs gives a fascinating insight into the dramatic changes that have occurred in central London over the last 150 years. The photographs provide a graphic impression of generations of people who lived and worked here in the late nineteenth and early twentieth centuries, and they recall houses and public buildings, shops, businesses and pubs that have vanished or been changed almost beyond recognition.

The book displays pictures taken by early photographers whose pioneering work added a new dimension to our record of the past and brings it vividly back to life. Their pictures show changing types of transport and fashion, and the evolving character of streets and districts as they took on the form that is familiar today.

Most aspects of daily life are recalled – hospitals and schools, work and recreation, shopping, church-going and the world wars. But the photographs also remember many famous national events – funerals, demonstrations, coronations – when the nation's attention was focused on Westminster.

Jill Barber has chosen a memorable selection of rare photographs from the City of Westminster Archives Centre to produce this sympathetic and revealing account of the recent past in the historic centre of the capital. Her book will add to the knowledge, appreciation and enjoyment of all those who take an interest in the development of this remarkable area and in the history of London as a whole.

Cover illustrations. Front: the Strand, 1913.
Back: sheltering in the tube, 1940.

£9.99
ISBN 0-7509-1721-0

9 780750 917216

CITY OF WESTMINSTER

SUTTON PUBLISHING LIMITED
PHOENIX MILL · STROUD · GLOUCESTERSHIRE

The Prestige Series
Venture Transport
of Consett

G E Hutchinson F.C.I.T., F.I.L.T.

Number Nineteen in The Prestige Series

from Venture

Series Editor: John Banks

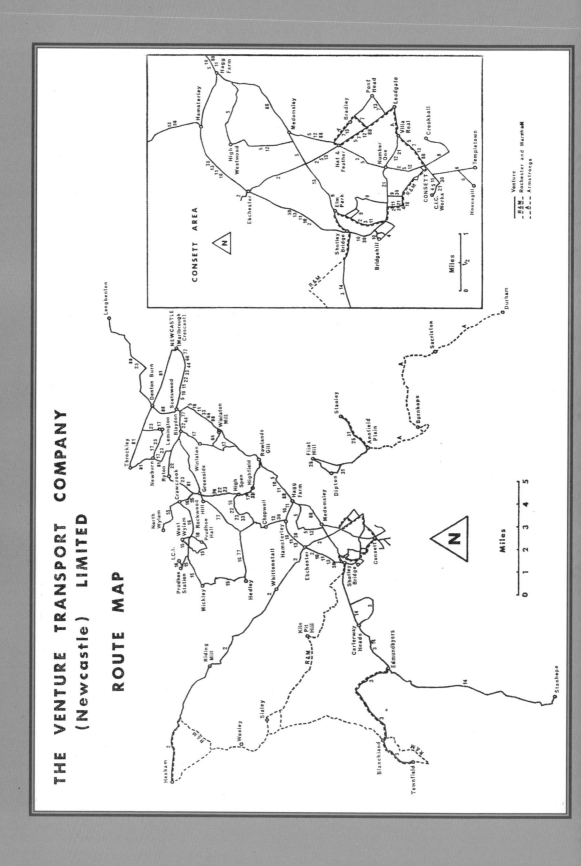

THE VENTURE TRANSPORT COMPANY (Newcastle) LIMITED

ROUTE MAP